heads of Leadenhall Market, and it's why streets with names like Addle Hill still lead to churches with names like St Andrew's-by-the-Wardrobe. Amongst all the noise and traffic the wraiths of the past still silently beckon from across the street.

It could be a baroque Thames embarkation point marooned in a little public park over 300 feet from the river and there are the little pavilions with railway destinations incised into their stones, which are the only reminder of the classical airs and graces of the original Euston Station. Or that precursor of the cinema, the Diorama, tucked away out of sight near Regent's Park. Unheeded and unsung, these ghosts and remnants from the past can still yield their pleasures if we just scratch the surface a little.

I was very fortunate that my scratching unearthed a very rich seam indeed. In the 1940s an artist called Peter Jackson drew a cartoon strip for *The Evening News*. 'Cartoon' is slightly misleading as these were superbly illustrated panels called 'London is Stranger than Fiction' and 'London Explorer' that brought together fascinating and preposterous facts about the capital. Some of the entries smacked of Mr Jackson making notes late at night in noisy pubs, such as the one about the Edmonton hen that laid an egg with an inscription on it warning of an imminent earthquake, but for the most part his strip was a catalogue of genuine oddities, collected magpie-like into his Kensington studio. Mercifully these strips were later collated into book form and one dark winter's afternoon I fell on a pair of them in a dimly-lit junk shop in Deptford. Anyone can get their hands on a website, but the pleas near the glory of stum sill of a dusty bookshop.

Of course treasures like these London Peculiars can't just be jottings copied slavishly from other people's endeavours. The most rewarding aspect of collecting is discovering things for one's self. Many of the curiosities pictured here are the result of my seeing something slightly odd out of the corner of my eye and then finding out about it. And, of course, once everyone heard what I was up to I was, if not deluged, then well-watered with suggestions. It was as a result of one of these in particular, down on the 'Greenwich Peninsula', that I realised that London Peculiars aren't just the oddities that have survived from the capital's past. New curiosities are appearing all the time, like alien spacecraft that after a while start sending out signals to those of us with an inquisitive nature.

### Author's Note

All of these Peculiars are easily accessible. All you will need is an A to Z or equivalent, a good Underground map and a stout pair of shoes. As you walk about you will, as I did, see other curiosities. Indeed you may know of many more that I missed (I know I've only seen a tiny fraction) and I would be very grateful to know about them via the publisher. I've concentrated on the plethora of candidates in the City and Westminster, and now I really want to get to grips with outer London, particularly the south.

overground underground

**EISENHOWER SHELTER, CHENIES STREET**  🚇 Goodge Street

Wartime sent London underground. The Cabinet War Rooms, with their green Bakelite telephones and maps studded with giant pins, are the most well-known example of a secret underground control centre for a government soldiering-on out of sight of Nazi bomb aimers. However, numerous deep subterranean office blocks existed all over the capital.

Here in Chenies Street off Tottenham Court Road these imposing blockhouses, now got up like fancy cakes, mark the entrance to General Eisenhower's headquarters from where, as Allied Supreme Commander, he directed the D-Day landings. It was connected to the Cabinet War Rooms by a pneumatic dispatch tube. The government still keeps a clause in the current tenancy agreements that means it can take them over again at very short notice should national security demand it.

## HAWKSMOOR CONDUIT, GREENWICH PARK

⇌ Greenwich, Maze Hill

Greenwich Park is riddled with subterranean passages and conduits. An elaborate conduit head sits hidden on the western side of the park. It's called the Hawksmoor Conduit, although we can't be absolutely sure that Nicholas Hawksmoor designed it himself. However, he was Clerk of Works to Greenwich Hospital from 1698 to 1735, so this and the little Hyde Vale conduit would certainly have been his responsibility and one can't imagine Hawksmoor not putting in his sovereign's worth.

This building obviously needed to make more of a statement about the benefits of water supply and looks remarkably like the entrance to a nonconformist chapel. Like all buildings either built by or associated with Hawksmoor, who was Christopher Wren's assistant for many years, it has a powerful and brooding presence. Here under the vault of trees the quasi-religious feel is emphasised by the curved wall behind the front elevation being very reminiscent of the semicircular apses rounding-off a chancel behind the altar.

**CONDUIT, HYDE VALE, GREENWICH** ⇌ Greenwich

A beautiful piece of half-domed brickwork stands at the top of Hyde Vale
between Blackheath and the outer fringes of Greenwich Park, a conduit head
that once sent water down the hill to the Greenwich Hospital on the
waterfront below. It was probably erected in 1710 and was fully restored in
2002 by The Freshwater Group of Companies and English Heritage. It is a
happy example of looking after the smaller buildings that are so much part of
our past but that nevertheless have an unnerving habit of getting overlooked.

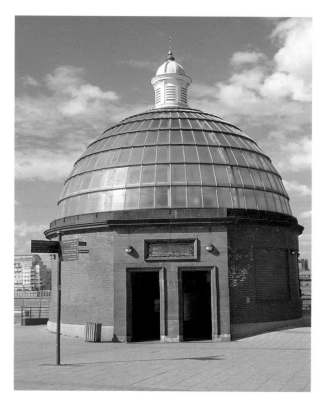

## GREENWICH FOOT TUNNEL ⇌ Greenwich

In 1902 *The Illustrated London News* welcomed the Greenwich Foot Tunnel with drawings of Edwardian Londoners flocking to try out the new subterranean wonder under the River Thames. The entrances are brick pagodas topped with glass domes and cupolas, and inside each a mahogany-veneered lift descends to where 200,000 white glazed tiles line a 1,217ft-long tunnel. At midstream at high tide the tunnel is 53 feet under water. The entrance on the north bank is in Island Gardens, a little oasis of greenery at the foot of the Isle of Dogs, the best viewpoint for the magnificent Greenwich Hospital across the Thames. Pedestrians emerge from the south bank entrance onto a breezy piazza shared with the *Cutty Sark* and Francis Chichester's diminutive *Gipsy Moth IV*.

The 1903 London County Council by-laws were keen that no person should attempt the crossing under the influence of alcohol, and that 'No person shall spit on or upon the tunnel or its approaches, stairs, lift, passages, or other means of ingress or egress thereto or therefrom.'

## GIBSON SQUARE, ISLINGTON  ⊖ Angel

A classical park pavilion is found amongst the lawns and roses of Gibson Square. The dome in this case is an open mesh, for this is a ventilator shaft terminal for the Victoria Line underneath. The architect was Quinlan Terry, who, I think, argues that the classical orders of architecture were handed down by God as a sort of appendix to the Ten Commandments. Terry's practice with fellow classicist Raymond Erith produced beautiful pieces of artwork to demonstrate their buildings.  He naturally called his 1969 ventilator the Tower of the Winds.

## MEMORIAL, CLOAK LANE ⊖ Cannon Street

A glance at the map will show that the stations of Mansion House and Cannon Street are aligned on the surface with Cloak Lane. A few yards down the street on the north side is this curious monument offset from the pavement. It tells of a sad detail in the construction of the District Railway, not of the death of those working on the line, but of the disinterment of human remains that had lain in expectancy of everlasting peace, some for 400 years, in the churchyard of St John the Baptist. The church was once on the banks of one of London's lost rivers, the Walbrook, which flowed past its west wall, and was one of the many churches destroyed in the Great Fire.

Nothing could stop the progress of London's railway system, not even the dead, so, as the monument tells us, the remains were 'carefully collected and reinterred in a vault beneath…'. As you stand on the pavement reading the inscription you will be only too aware of the sound of trains rumbling by just a few feet away.

## COAL HOLE, PARK SQUARE EAST ⊖ Regent's Park

Coal hole plates are as ubiquitous in London as cast-iron manhole covers, their larger counterparts. To test the veracity of a coal hole one must look beyond the pavement to the frontage of the adjoining house. If there is a basement area reached by steps, chances are a coal store will be underneath the pavement or, of course, less noticeably, there will be a cellar underneath the house. Either way these plates are covering access holes through which coal can be delivered without disturbing the household, lessening the frequency of fraternisation between Fred the coalman and Polly the cook's maid.

## SACRED

TO THE MEMORY OF THE

# DEAD

INTERRED IN THE ANCIENT CHURCH & CHURCHYARD

## OF St JOHN THE BAPTIST

UPON WALBROOK

DURING FOUR CENTURIES.

THE FORMATION OF THE DISTRICT RAILWAY

HAVING NECESSITATED THE DESTRUCTION OF

THE GREATER PART OF THE

# CHURCHYARD

ALL THE HUMAN REMAINS CONTAINED THEREIN

ERE CAREFULLY COLLECTED AND REINTERRED

## FOOT TUNNEL ENTRANCES, RICHMOND AND TWICKENHAM ⇄ Richmond

A walk down Old Palace Lane in Richmond is to walk through quintes-
sential England. It is the kind of image you see in post-war black-and-white
picture books, brought out in colour: orange brick, creamy stuccos and
brilliant white woodwork broken up by laurels and neat privet. There's an
almost Arts-and-Crafts motor garage that must have once cossetted the
coachwork of early Lagondas and Derby Bentleys, and if the thought of it
all gets a bit too much there's a little pub serving London beer on wooden
tables. If you do manage to get any further, there's a pair of hidden
treasures by the river at the end of the lane.

Twickenham Bridge was only built in 1933, as all attempts to cross the
river at this point had been thwarted because any approach to it would
mean cutting through the Old Deer Park. But there was a foot tunnel and
here in the shadows is one of the entrances. Someone who works on the

river locally told me that it's still possible to crawl through it, but the thought sends shivers down my spine as surely as ice cold water would drip down one's neck in the darkness.

The curious pepper pot building is carefully built in brick with a tiled roof and a little metal ventilator on top like a tiny castle turret. The heavily padlocked green door is set in a Gothic arch and is hung with a pair of seductive wrought iron hinges. It has a very forlorn look about it. On the opposite bank its companion also sits alone, surrounded by snatching brambles and white trumpets of bindweed, identical in all things except there's more fencing to stop you getting near it. The passage of the tunnel lies between the 1908 railway bridge, with the trains thundering over the houseboats on its open steel spandrels, and the modernist Twickenham Bridge with bronze handrails lining the steps that climb up from the towpaths to the roaring main road.

## LEINSTER GARDENS, BAYSWATER
⊖ Bayswater

The postman knocks in vain at the doors of 23–4 Leinster Gardens, where the glass and woodwork of sightless windows are only grey and white paint. No twitching curtains, no lamps lit at dusk, for what you see here is literally all there is.

In the late 1860s the Metropolitan Railway extended their operations west from Edgware Road to Gloucester Road. Early underground railway engineering was 'cut-and-cover', which meant that instead of deep tube tunnelling, cuttings were excavated at the surface and then covered over. This method facilitated a wider, airier environment, essential when the locomotive power was still based on steam. So the Metropolitan cut and covered its way through the quiet streets of Paddington and Bayswater, fully expecting to pull down a section of stuccoed terrace in Leinster Gardens. But the locals were enraged that their street should suffer such an indignity and demanded that the frontages of the houses concerned should be retained, keeping up appearances at street level at least.

So now the trains serving the District and Circle Lines trundle underneath, their passengers unaware of the film set deceit above their heads. Up in Leinster Gardens one of two hotels next door joins in the fun by extending their balcony flowers in front of the neighbouring *trompe l'oeil* windows. Probationers from Paddington Green Police Station are sent round to conduct spurious enquiries while their senior officers presumably hide round the corner chuckling to themselves.

## THE WESTBOURNE RIVER AT SLOANE SQUARE UNDERGROUND STATION ⊖ Sloane Square

Although for the most part invisible, the Westbourne still makes its presence felt not only in a handful of names given to streets and terraces, but in some very unlikely venues. The river rises on Hampstead Heath up by Jack Straw's Castle, winding its way underground through Kilburn, under the Westway flyover and the main railway tracks at Paddington until it bursts out into the open in Hyde Park. Here a succession of ponds fed by the river were dammed in 1730 by Queen Caroline, the wife of George II, forming what we now know as the Serpentine. It once flowed out of Hyde Park under Knight's Bridge – infamous as the haunt of highwaymen – but now it becomes subterranean posh as it skirts Belgravia, dividing into two streams under Chelsea Barracks before decanting into the Thames.

But let's just move back upstream a little and go down onto the platforms of Sloane Square Underground Station. It's here we can look up and see a massive iron trough crossing the tracks of the District and Circle Lines. This is the Westbourne, hidden from view but still flowing determinedly across west London.

## TOWER SUBWAY, TOWER HILL ⊖ Tower Hill

This rotund little building is the entrance to the only privately-owned tunnel under the Thames. Now carrying cable television trunking, it was once the very first underground railway in the world. It opened in 1870 with a 12-passenger cable car service that trundled under the river from Tower Hill to Vine Lane, on the opposite bank near Tooley Street. The project gave birth to the Greathead Shield, a tunnelling device that was a similar but more sophisticated version of Marc Brunel's Rotherhithe Tunnel shipworm-style boring machine. It was named after the engineer James Henry Greathead.

The subway only operated for a few months, but until Tower Bridge opened it enjoyed considerable success as a foot tunnel, pedestrians descending by steam lifts situated in both this entrance and its companion in Vine Lane.

## THE MILLENNIUM DOME, MILLENNIUM WAY, GREENWICH ⊖ North Greenwich

There are many peculiar things about the Millennium Dome, but all of that nonsense is a distraction from the thing itself. Coming down from Silvertown to the Blackwall Tunnel it looks like a beautiful spaceship has landed legs-up next to the Thames. And quite a sizeable spaceship at that. Somewhere I learnt that you could put the Great Pyramid of Giza inside it, which would certainly have been a better idea then what they actually did put in it, but that pecularity is not why it has found a home in these pages.

If you look at a street map of London you'll notice that the southbound Blackwall Tunnel (separated from its northbound counterpart by about an eighth of a mile) is only under the Thames for less than half its overall length. That's because it needs a good run at it, and conversely, as it ascends up onto the Greenwich Peninsula (marketing-speak for Bugsby's Marshes) it needs to do a sharp right-hander in order to run down to Woolwich. It's still a quarter of a mile from fresh air so there has to be a ventilator, coincidentally where they decided to build the Dome. So that big depression on its south-west corner is to accommodate a white chimney that releases traffic exhaust out over the Millennium Greenwich Village.

street life

## THE TRAFALGAR SQUARE POLICE STATION
⊖ Charing Cross

Auxiliary police stations have all but disappeared from the London scene. Once, the Metropolitan copper on the beat kept in touch with his nick from strategically-placed miniature offices. The police box crowned with its flashing blue light is still familiar to us, but only because it's the transport-of-choice for Doctor Who.

Evidence can still be found of these outposts and here in the south-east corner of Trafalgar Square is a particularly well-disguised example. It is hollowed out from one of four lamp pillars that sit at the extremities of the square. There's just about room for an average-sized policeman and his truncheon, but on my visit I was disappointed to find the lantern base now functioning as a refuge for the Square's cleaners and their *Sun* newspapers. The polygonal bronze lantern is not, as London myth would have it, one of a series taken from Nelson's flagship *Victory*. The panopticon design is unique to the lamps in the square, believed by its designer to provide, like a diamond, more light from its multiple refraction.

## BOLLARD, GRACECHURCH STREET
⊖ Monument

This bollard is classic City of London street hardware, painted in what are almost the corporate colours of this kind of thing, perhaps taking a cue from the white-striping used during wartime blackout conditions for hazard warnings in the darkened streets. This proud chap sits on a tiny traffic island where Gracechurch Street meets Eastcheap, surrounded by plainer fellows and topped out with what looks like a giant lemon squeezer. My first thought was that it was a particularly robust example to stop wayward trams hurtling precipitously down the steps of the adjoining underground lavatory, but closer inspection revealed a cut-out fretwork grille on each side. I am now reliably informed by a drain savant at the Corporation that it is simply a bollard that doubles-up as a ventilator for the same toilets.

## PATENT SEWER VENTILATING LAMP, CARTING LANE ⊖ Charing Cross

Geoffery Fletcher, in *The London Nobody Knows*, says of this curiosity at the side of the Savoy Hotel '…I often tremble for its future.' That was in 1962 and I too trembled as I descended the steps down from the Strand into Carting Lane. But I cheered to myself when it became immediately apparent that not only had the Patent Sewer Ventilating Lamp survived, but it was glowing greenly with gas. Whether it was running on excess gas from the sewers was uncertain, but if not then somebody needs to be applauded for saving this London Peculiar and connecting it up to the mains.

The column is hollow, designed to allow sewer vapours to ascend to the lantern where it was safely burnt off, conveniently lighting the street at the same time. It is a gentle reminder that once all of London was lit by these calm, pale lights, the perfect stage lighting for some of the darker Victorian preoccupations. As Mr Fletcher quotes:

Underneath the gaslight's glitter
Stands a little fragile girl
Heedless of the night winds bitter
As they round about her whirl…

### HOUSES OF PARLIAMENT TAXI LIGHT, PARLIAMENT SQUARE ⊖ Westminster

A little lamp sits on top of a stone pillar at the corner of Parliament Square and Bridge Street. If you're a taxi driver passing by and you notice the lamp is flashing you can do a quick U-turn and pick up a fare from the Houses of Parliament. MPs can ask the constable at the Members' Gate for the light to be switched on when their departure is imminent. Alternatively the light can act as a warning beacon to cabbies not taken to discoursing with politicians.

### LAMP-POST, BRUNSWICK PLACE ⊖ Regent's Park

It seems remarkable that the monarch most associated with this area – at least in his Regency – is still commemorated with his cipher on something as simple as a lamp-post. I assume it has been here in Brunswick Place, to the south of Regent's Park, for at least 170 years: shining palely on ladies and gentlemen alighting from coaches, hansoms and broughams; blacked-out in wartime; a useful support for revellers in victory celebrations.

## BLUE POST, EASTCHEAP

I took this photograph back in the late 1980s and thought I'd better check it out before including it in this book. It's a perfect example of a simple column that once held a telephone for use by constables on their beats in the City of London. A little light flashed on and off to alert them to incoming calls. Sadly, all that remains is a little patch of tarmac on the pavement. I wonder why it couldn't have been left here; even if it was no longer required for police duties its purpose could have been set out on a little plaque for the future education of those who grew up without these unassuming but bright little pieces of street furniture.

### OUTER CIRCLE, REGENT'S PARK
⊖ Regent's Park

This bollard is gradually disappearing into the hedgerow ivy on
the eastern side of Regent's Park. Nearby another bollard is
painted black and of nondescript design, but this example is a
fat piece of domed granite with a letter 'S' cut into it. What can
it mean? My first guess was that the 'S' was a service indicator
for a nearby sewer hatch, but in fact it is a boundary marker
between the parishes of St Marylebone and St Pancras.

### VICTUALLING YARD, GROVE STREET
⇌ Deptford

Many London bollards are pointed out as being
recycled from old cannon, topped-out with a
cannon ball in the muzzle. Well, most of them
aren't. But here, outside the 1788 gateway to what
remains of the Royal Navy's Victualling Yard, are the
real things, an impressively heavy gun salute in a
Deptford side street.

**BOUNDARY MARKER, EAST HEATH ROAD, HAMPSTEAD**

⊖ Hampstead

Positioned at just the right height for tying up a shoelace or catching you just below the knee in the fog, this cast-iron bollard sits on Preacher's Hill to the west of Hampstead Ponds. So much better than the modern equivalents that have to gush some doubtful council virtue: 'working so hard for you' etc, this marker just tells us that this is where the London County Council started its jurisdiction. No nonsense, plain embossed letters on a seductive shape.

**BOLLARD, PETO PLACE**

⊖ Regent's Park

This bollard is a Queen Elizabeth II version with neatly scored horizontal bands. With its companion opposite it stands ready to take the sides off vans attempting to negotiate the narrow confines of Peto Place. The flowers behind are a very welcome break to the tedium of Marylebone Road, a little fecund garden in front of a terrace of stucco houses.

## SAND BIN, TEMPLE PLACE  ⊖ Temple

This is the sort of thing you'd expect to score fifty points for in an I-Spy book. It took a long time to get to know all about this impressive item of street furniture, but eventually I got an exhaustive account from deep within the heart of Westminster Council. This actual example may well be a more recent replica, but the originals, of which there is only a handful left, were designed in Edwardian times as sand bins. The idea was that sand was shovelled from a wagon into the top and was then gravity-fed to an aperture at the base where the council's workmen could slide out shovelfuls for distribution over the street. The survivors are often in a heritage colour scheme of black and gold, like litter bins and some phone boxes, but I also remember seeing them in heraldic silver in the past.

We are familiar with ugly fat plastic grit boxes at the side of roads, but the use of sand from these bins was far more in keeping with London life. Sand would often be spread across the carriageway to muffle the sound of horses' hooves outside houses where the family was in mourning, or even at the request of doctors for silence when a patient's critical illness demanded it. But the most common usage is ceremonial. Sand was – and still is – spread out to give processional horses a better grip on improved road surfaces and for making street cleaning after these events more effective.

## PORTER'S REST, PICCADILLY

⊖ Hyde Park Corner

This curious item of street furniture is on the south side of Piccadilly where the slip road connects to Hyde Park Corner, just before the underpass. It is the only surviving example of a porter's rest that I know of, and its preservation is remarkable. Before mechanised transport, goods were carried on pack mules and horse-drawn wagons, but large loads would also be carried on the bent backs of men. This wooden shelf, supported on two cast-iron pillars, is positioned at exactly the right height for a porter to turn and rest his pack without taking it off his back.

By the mid-19th century these conveniences were fast disappearing and in 1861 the MP for Shrewsbury, R L Slaney, suggested that '…this porter's rest be erected…by the Vestry of St George, Hanover Square for the benefit of porters and others carrying burdens, as a relic of a past world in London's history…. It is hoped that the people will aid its preservation.' Today it is more likely to be the resting place for a hot styrene coffee cup than a colporteur's pack of bibles, but it is nevertheless still a welcome addition to the busy Piccadilly streetscape.

**DRINKING TROUGH, WEST CARRIAGE DRIVE, HYDE PARK**  ⊖ South Kensington (Science Museum exit)

These coffin-shaped lumps of granite are perhaps the item of street furniture most taken for granted, such is their ubiquity. They were once the equivalent of our filling stations, a ready supply of fresh water for the hundreds of thousands of horses (and cattle) that filled the streets of London until motor engine exhaust replaced the heady perfume of recently-released dung. By 1885, 50,000 horses were drinking from London troughs alone.

The prime mover in providing clean drinking water for animals (and the public) was the Metropolitan Drinking Fountain and Cattle Trough Association. Until their endeavours started to bear fruit it had not been unusual for cattle to be driven down the drovers' roads of Britain for days on end in summer heat without a proper water supply. Although some troughs benefited from the Victorian desire to add decoration, most are this simple unadulterated shape, with perhaps just a text along the lines of 'A righteous man regardeth the life of his beast.'

## FERRYMAN'S SEAT, BEAR GARDENS, SOUTHWARK ⊖ Southwark

The name 'Bear Gardens' will immediately conjure up some fairly brutish imagery and Southwark had one of the most famous bear-baiting pits in England, opened on Bankside in 1526. John Evelyn recorded in his diary that this was undoubtedly 'a rude and dirty pastime', but it continued to be legal until it was finally abolished in 1835. Now the only reminders in Southwark are the street name and this curious ledge near the corner with Bankside.

Southwark was always seen as outlaw country. The presence of a cathedral that looks as if it should be in the Cotswolds and the still magnificent Borough Market are testament to the growth of an alternative society on the South Bank. London jealously guarded its mercantile life and those barred from bringing their goods across London Bridge soon set up their stalls outside the jurisdiction of the merchant guilds. So Southwark became the place to go for dodgy pastimes and the black market, and the convenience of a river ferry supplemented the bridge. This stone ledge is the original ferryman's seat where he would have waited for bear-baiting fans to decant from the gardens in order to return to the north shore. It looks highly polished, as if rubbed smooth by roughly-woven trousers, and has a slightly worrying hole in the seat, but its very survival is remarkable, having been placed in the wall of a succession of buildings on this site.

## THE CITY OF LONDON'S COMMEMORATIVE PLAQUES, COLLEGE HILL

⊖ Cannon Street

The square mile of the City of London has always set itself aside from the London that developed outside its walls and jurisdiction. It has its own mayor, street bollards and police force. And you won't find any traditional blue plaques fastened on to the homes and workplaces of the famous dead, because the City goes its own way to mark the personal heritage of its citizens. These two plaques are very near each other on College Hill, celebrating places in the life of the bell-listening, feline-loving, four times Lord Mayor of London, Dick Whittington. His history can be found elsewhere; the Peculiars in this case are the plaques themselves.

Commemorative stoneware plaques were produced in a variety of designs by Doulton in their Lambeth works, including the much more well-known circular blue plaques that appear elsewhere in London. I actually prefer the City variety for the rich detailing that includes the City badge, the use of such a full-on glossy glaze and the fact that they are often about historical sites as much as the rich and famous, but I suppose the circular plaques are far more adaptable to different building types and materials. Until the Lambeth works closure in 1956, Doulton maintained an office just to look after commemorative work, which usually focused on designs for the more common celebratory mugs and jugs for which they are well known, but also dealt with the plaques for the City.

**WAYSIDE MADONNA, O'MEARA STREET** ⊖ Borough

Walking down O'Meara Street this serene wayside Madonna comes as
an unexpected antidote to the teeming life of Southwark, particularly
with the thunderous clattering of trains overhead, their wheels singing
like bacon slicers. The little shrine's close proximity to the roadway and
the cast-iron bridge is only accentuated by the choice of a seaside
colours paint scheme and the lovingly-tended pelargoniums. It is the
kind of thing we would expect to see at a rural French crossroads.

The Church of the Precious Blood is at its side and, although very
distinctive with its twin Italianate towers, it perhaps shrinks a little into
anonymity by comparison. But walk inside and, although you are
greeted by a wonderfully light, white-painted interior, it is still a space of
friendly warmth and calm. The terracotta Stations of the Cross were
made in Belgium and hauled here from the docks by the parishioners.

# roupell street

## ROUPELL STREET ⊖ Southwark

London's railway termini form their own hinterlands, owing much to the fact that the buildings disgorge an unceasing tide of people into the city every day. Walk around Waterloo Station and the evidence is clear: businesses in railway arches, a terracotta-clad hospital, the monolithic Shell buildings. The terminus is at the heart of matters, influencing everything within its aura.

Tucked-up near to the railway lines that rumble through Waterloo East is a remarkable survivor from the early 19th century, a street of modest cottages that immediately evokes another London, the London of self-contained workers' communities. Although the houses are in a terrace, each has its gable turned end-on to the street and a front door painted an individual (but nevertheless harmonious) colour. Halfway down is a friendly corner pub where I once sat and watched black-suited commuters hurrying to Waterloo through the rain from the City and Blackfriars Bridge. The scene looked like a smudged Lowry painting. Near the end of Roupell Street, Theed Street – similarly heart-warming in character – curves off and one can see a little building that proves how communities can adapt and still retain their character. Starting life as a church hall it later became a motor engineer's; now it's an acupuncture centre.

Ian Nairn loved this street. To quote from his inimitable *Nairn's London:* 'On one level, there is no finer architectural effect in London; on another there is no better sense of place in London. And the whole lot is truly humble and all screwed into the big city.'

on the waterfront

**TIDE KIOSK, WESTMINSTER BRIDGE** ⊖ Westminster

This octagonal copper structure must be one of the most ignored little buildings in London. Thousands of tourists pass by it on their way up the steps from the Embankment to Westminster Bridge. Sitting in a corner, perched on the balustrade above the river in the shadow of Boudicca's chariot, it offers no clue as to its use and the tiny apertures in the sides hardly pass as windows. However, its purpose is both simple and unromantic: hiding in its dark recesses are instruments that were used for measuring the tides.

A contemporary account of tide gauges from the 1930s says 'A float is attached by wire via geared wheels to a recording pen which marks the tidal variations on a sheet of paper placed around a horizontal drum completely revolved every 24 hours by a clock.' The gauges were checked every day and were also used to predict tidal surges.

**OBELISK, RIVER THAMES, NEAR TEDDINGTON LOCK** ⇌ Teddington

Hidden amongst the riverside trees and undergrowth near Teddington Lock is this little obelisk on the Ham shore. It looks like a simple churchyard memorial or village market cross, but it is in fact a boundary marker denoting the extent of the jurisdiction of two river authorities. There had always been arguments about who was responsible for what on the Thames – the locks, the weirs, the fishing rights – but the problems were mostly sorted out when Teddington Lock was installed in 1811 to form the furthest reach of the tidal Thames.

Downstream of this obelisk was the responsibility of the Port of London Authority, upstream that of the Thames Conservancy. The difference in character is quite marked. Downstream the river is urbane and business-like, with commerce crowding to the water's edge and the hint of ozone on the tidal mud. Upstream is rural England: overhanging trees, rowing skiffs and the ghosts of Jerome K Jerome's *Three Men in a Boat* trying to get to sleep under the stars.

## LONDON BRIDGE ALCOVE, GUY'S HOSPITAL, ST THOMAS STREET
London Bridge

As we use London Bridge to cross over the Thames between Southwark and the City, the bridge beneath our feet (or tyres) is of late 1960s vintage. The first known bridge at this point was a wooden Roman affair, about 200 yards to the east, but timber structures here were replaced by the spectacular outline of the first stone bridge, opened in 1209, with its rows of houses ranging across 19 arches. Amazingly, these buildings, familiar from so many prints and paintings, survived until the mid-18th century, when Robert Taylor and George Dance removed them and also replaced a very medieval drawbridge with a central navigation span.

But what has all that got to with this humpbacked shelter in the middle of a lawn at Guy's Hospital? Well, once Taylor and Dance had removed the houses, they placed stone alcoves, complete with seats, on top of each pier of the original bridge. One imagines them to have been quickly and gratefully utilised by footpads and prostitutes. When the inevitable road-widening occurred in the early 20th century, the alcoves were removed; however, three survived: one to rest here for the use of doctors and nurses and two that were carted out to Victoria Park in Hackney.

## THE 1864 BLACKFRIARS RAILWAY BRIDGE ⊖ Blackfriars

Protruding up from the Thames next to Blackfriars railway bridge is a series of deep pink clusters of columns with foliate heads that are the remains of another bridge on this site; until the removal of the five latticed girder spans it was the oldest extant crossing downstream of Battersea. Joseph Cubitt and F T Turner built it for the London, Chatham & Dover Railway and it is this company's insignia that form such a show-stopping end to the series of redundant piers.

This giant badge is one of the most fabulous pieces of public heraldry in existence and we are indeed lucky that it wasn't consigned to a scrap heap when the bridge was taken down. The integral coats of arms are, clockwise from the top: Kent, Dover, Rochester and the City of London. The railway served most of Kent and the Channel ports and takes its motto from Kent's 'invincible' white horse. The name *Invicta* was used for the first steam locomotive to run in Kent, also becoming the first engine to travel through a railway tunnel.

## RICHMOND HALF-TIDE WEIR AND FOOTBRIDGE,
## RANELAGH DRIVE ⊖ Richmond

The tidal Thames has 28 crossings between Teddington Weir and the
Tower of London. There are railway bridges that we scarcely notice
unless we walk under them on a riverside path as a train thunders
over, while Hammersmith, Albert and Tower Bridges have undisputed
charms in terms of extravagant decoration. However, my clear
favourite is this wonderfully eclectic concoction of Victorian steel,
ironwork and deep orange bricks.

The London Bridge of 1832 caused the river between Teddington and
Richmond to reduce to a meandering trickle at low tide, sometimes
only 18 inches deep. To maintain a navigable waterway, a set of three
sluice gates was included inside the steel arches of this bridge and
these could be lowered on the falling tide. This action keeps a depth of
at least five feet of water upstream and is an impressive sight for
anyone lucky enough to be on one of the two footbridges at the time.

The bridge arrived here in 1894, the result of vigorous campaigning by
Mr Hilditch of Richmond and the ingenuity of an Irish engineer,
Mr F G M Stoney. And what a pleasure it is. The bridge is approached
on the Twickenham side by Ranelagh Drive, a little tree-lined
embankment where fishermen set up their rods on the wide
pavement and au pair girls buy ice cream for their charges from a
gently humming van. Flights of steps on brick supports bring you onto
one of two footbridges, everything edged with mint-coloured posts
and rails supporting the buttermilk quatre-foiled parapets. Every now
and then a fancy lamp standard holds up a glass globe. The best is last:
a lead-roofed pavilion with a railway valance and a clock to time the
tide by. Look over the balustrade and you see that this is just the top
storey of an abutment in blue engineering brick housing the Port of
London Authority office. If the sluice gates are down, then you and
your boat will go through the lock where a fee is collected in a bucket
let down from above.

### YORK WATER GATE, VICTORIA EMBANKMENT GARDENS  Embankment

On John Rocque's map of Georgian London, Buckingham Street is shown coming down to the River Thames from the Strand, finishing at the water's edge at York Buildings Stairs. The engraved lines of the rippling river can be seen lapping at an indication of steps running down into the water. An archway was built here to provide an embarkation point from the gardens of the Duke of Buckingham's mansion, constructed in 1626. The archway was left standing when the house was demolished 50 years later and it is still there, a wonderful showpiece for the baroque with lots of rustication and sculptured nauticalia, reflecting its original purpose.

However, this isn't a monument that has been taken down piece by piece and removed from the river's edge to become an agreeable diversion in a public park. No, it's the river that moved. The York Water Gate is exactly where it's always been, it's present position the result of Sir Joseph Bazalgette's construction of the Victoria Embankment between 1864 and 1870, which created a new shoreline some distance away. If one ignores the pathetic little flower pots in front of it, something of its busy grandeur still remains in the shadow of the trees: the shouts from watermen as they jostled for position, the flashing of brightly coloured silks as the Duke of Buckingham and his entourage flounced their way onto a decorative barge.

## GRAIN ELEVATOR, NORTH WOOLWICH ROAD
**DLR** Prince Regent

When I was a small child in the 1950s I vividly remember being taken on a boat trip downstream on the River Thames. In particular I recall seeing the seemingly endless docks and wharves with tall cranes swinging cargo up from the holds of steam ships and men shouting to each other from high up on the wooden ledges of warehouse openings. It was a world of intense activity and excitement, noisy with the blasts of horns and the constant clanking of chains. Black tugs with red funnels fussed in and out of billows of white steam and I felt a little frightened to see things so foreign to my rural sensibilities.

Most of it has now disappeared. Containerisation meant that the traditional dockers and their swinging cranes were no longer needed and the docks became scenes of dereliction, divided up by vast and empty sheets of water. Until, of course, the developers moved in to do lunchtime presentations on motor yachts.

Occasional reminders of the original dockland industries can still be found amongst the office buildings and 'lifestyle' apartments. Out in North Woolwich the Royal Victoria Dock was once home to Spiller's Millennium Mills and in the past a row of grain elevators on Pontoon Dock groped in the bowels of ships for imported grain that was milled for an ever-increasing London market. All has now been sterilised, with 'corporate hospitality functions' reached by roads lined with maintenance-free shrubs set in bark chippings. But there is one survivor from the Pontoon Dock, peering over the trees and gardens like a lost white-shrouded giant: a grain elevator, signed with the letter 'D' to guide its next cargo to the correct berth. A cargo that may now prove to be somewhat elusive.

## LAMBETH BRIDGE PINEAPPLES ⊖ Westminster

Lambeth Bridge is an unremarkable London County Council structure of five steel arches, which was opened in 1932 a little further upstream from its predecessor. But on the approaches are tall obelisks, each topped with a pineapple. Or are they?

The story starts nearby in the St Mary-at-Lambeth churchyard where three generations of the Tradescant family are buried. John Tradescant the Elder, who died in 1638, was the gardener for King Charles I; Tradescant the Younger worked for Charles II. Both were amongst the earliest collectors of natural curiosities. Their name has become inextricably linked with the introduction and subsequent cultivation of the pineapple and it has been assumed that these obelisks with their exotic fruits are reminders of this fact and the close proximity of the Tradescant burials.

We don't know whether either Tradescant had anything to do with pineapples, and certainly we know that the first cultivated one in Britain was presented to Charles II after the younger Tradescant's death. In any case these obelisk fruit don't even really look like pineapples (where are the spiky leaves on top?). That's because they're pine cones, a symbol of hospitality from at least Roman times. Their use as an architectural motif is widespread; one thinks of Georgian gate piers and railings in particular. The confusion lies in pine cones once being called pine apples, so that when the scaly fruit arrived looking vaguely similar the same name was adopted. So we really ought to think of Lambeth Bridge more fruitfully as the most welcoming bridge in London.

## VAUXHALL BRIDGE, LAMBETH ⊖ Vauxhall

Poking one's nose over bridge parapets is always a worthwhile occupation. One is confronted by curious things designed only to be seen by those traversing underneath and from equally curious perspectives. Vauxhall Bridge has had many manifestations on this site, but the present structure, which opened in 1906, is a straightforward affair from Alexander Binnie, who was also responsible for Highgate's Archway. However, on each of the eight piers (four each side) are bronze figures by Alfred Drury and F W Pomeroy. Most are fairly routine: symbolic females clasping utensils like urns to represent some higher meaning. But on the upstream side is something extraordinary. *Architecture* is symbolised not by rules and compasses, or beribboned scrolls, but by a perfectly detailed model of St Paul's Cathedral cradled in the hand of one of the female figures. And for once the most advantageous view is obtained by cautiously leaning over the edge.

towering prospects

## SEVERNDROOG CASTLE, SHOOTERS HILL ROAD
≹ Eltham

Hidden in Castle Wood, just off the original Dover Road, this curious building was built in 1784 as a prospect tower by Lady James, to commemorate her husband Sir William's capture of an island off the coast of Malabar called Severndroog. Her architect, Richard Jupp, produced an ingenious design that looks like a traditional square tower but is in fact three-sided. It has the pretensions of a castle, but the views cry out for larger window openings and here was a fabulous opportunity to indulge the contemporary craze for the Gothic. The prospects are indeed stunning – wide sweeps of Kent, Surrey and Essex across the river. But most fascinating are the views of the city closer to hand, a slightly distorted perspective of Blackheath, and the Millennium Dome rising up through a fog of pollution over to the north-west.

Severndroog Castle can be reached on paths through the surrounding woods, but sadly it will be a little longer before the current restoration plans are complete enough to allow access. Many will remember its use as a tearoom; it was also utilised as an observation tower, a function it admirably performed during two world wars, particularly with the installation of radar equipment. One can appreciate its usefulness in plotting incoming Dorniers droning their way up the narrowing Thames Estuary.

## BRUCE CASTLE, LORDSHIP LANE, TOTTENHAM
≹ Bruce Grove

Bruce Castle – since 1906 a Haringey museum and archives department – is a breath of fresh air on Lordship Lane as the A10 works its way northwards. Its pretty tower and cupola is an eye-catcher certainly, but there's something more intriguing hiding in the shadows of the trees on the south-west corner.

This circular red brick tower has puzzled historians since at least 1700 when Lord Coleraine wrote that, although he kept the tower in good repair, he had no idea of its builder or use. Loosely dated to the late 15th–early 16th century, it is doubtless of Tudor origin. It has been described as having a military bearing, but I think it has more of the look of a conduit head or an impressive game larder.

### SHOOTER'S HILL WATER TOWER, ELTHAM ⇄ Eltham

In 1910 this hilltop position was the perfect excuse for the water company to indulge itself in this grandiose self-advertisement, as if to proclaim: 'Look at us, bringing you your fresh water.' And indeed they did. Costing £3,256, water was pumped up here from chalk wells in Orpington, to then fall by gravity to a pumping station in Well Hall Road.

This water tower, a glowering landmark for travellers on the Old Dover Road, commands the crest of a hill that rises steeply up from Blackheath. It is a wonderful octagon of multi-coloured brick, standing 500 feet above sea level and overlooking several counties. It has that same kind of faux medievalism about it that brings to mind William Morris's garlanded fantasies, with its pointed rooflines and castle pretensions. It is, of course, now slightly disfigured by the insensitive addition of mobile phone aerials, but we should at least be glad that the tower hasn't been replaced by a modern equivalent, which would very likely be a rendition of a science fiction fantasy involving a hollowed-out spaceship.

### HORNIMAN MUSEUM, LONDON ROAD, FOREST HILL ⇄ Forest Hill

The South Circular is not the most enchanting of London's roads, but it does have its moments. One of them is here on London Road, Forest Hill. The Horniman Museum and its gardens were donated to London County Council in 1902 by Frederick John Horniman MP. He had made his fortune from tea, and collections from his globetrotting formed the basis for this fascinating anthropological museum.

The Peculiar here has to be the clock tower, which is of that school of architectural thinking that says that buildings can actually be quite fun. There is something vaguely American about it, the way the smooth silver stone walls have radial corners that grow upwards to become four domed pinnacles gripping a circular cornice. Or an exercise in how to turn a square tower into a round one and tell the time while doing it.

### THE KING'S CROSS LIGHTHOUSE, PENTONVILLE ROAD
⊖ King's Cross St Pancras

Perched high above the incessant noise of traffic negotiating the corner of Gray's Inn Road and Pentonville Road is this curious feature, something you would expect to find at the end of a jetty in Portsmouth. I have been unable to find out anything really meaningful about this little prospect tower with portholes and a vertiginous balcony; all I have is a vague memory of some snippet of pub talk that involved a retired sea captain who, like Captain Boom in *Mary Poppins*, kept a telescoped eye on all the comings and goings at King's Cross Station below. The snippet didn't extend to whether he let off a cannon if he saw the wind changing on his battered weathervane.

## CALEDONIAN MARKET, MARKET ROAD, ISLINGTON

⊖ Caledonian Road

The echoes of this colossal cattle market are now barely to be heard. Turning into Market Road off Caledonian Road (just past the forbidding outlines of Pentonville Prison, another fugitive built on the fringe of the city) the first clue to the extent of the former activities here are the black-painted railings, supported by Grecian-style posts. I assume that each post originally had a cast-iron cow's or pig's head attached to it, but of course now all that's left are the fixing holes.

Rising up defiantly above the shrubberies is this clock tower. It once stood in the centre of the Metropolitan Cattle Market, which had the capacity in its iron sheds and stalls for 34,900 sheep, 6,616 bullocks, 1,425 calves and 900 pigs. A wonderful example of Italianate Baroque, the tower is now on the northern edge of the park, with talk of the rest of the area disappearing under housing. Patrolling police officers attest to the park still being utilised for bestial activities.

The market moved here from Smithfields in 1852, onto what was then Copenhagen Fields. Herds of beasts were driven here from all over Britain, the final destination after days and weeks of traversing lonely wide-verged drovers' roads. The drovers were accommodated in hostels, and four giant public houses stood at each corner of the market. A survivor still stands on the south-east angle; originally called The White Horse it still flaunts its bracketed cast-iron balcony from where ribald exchanges would doubtless have taken place between bulbous-nosed dealers and red-faced farmers. One can only imagine what went on inside, with the beer glasses and optics clinking as down below trains steamed up through the Copenhagen Tunnel to King's Cross.

The 15 acres of granite paving also saw another life as a pitch for pedlars, who gradually transmuted into the more familiar dealers in furniture and artefacts. After the Second World War their licence to trade was not renewed and all the chiffoniers and Staffordshire dogs decamped to Bermondsey and Tower Bridge Road, where it all still goes on.

PERTH.

PETERBORO.

PRESTON.

ROCHDALE.

small buildings, big ideas

SHREWSBURY.

**EUSTON STATION LODGES, EUSTON ROAD** ⊖ Euston

The demolition of Euston Arch in the early 1960s created a landmark in our appreciation of Victorian architecture. Despite widespread public protest and an offer from the demolition company to number and re-erect the stones at another site of the railway's choice, it was razed to the ground to make way for the new terminus.

The Greek Doric propylaeum was designed for the London & Birmingham Railway by Philip Hardwick and completed in 1838, a 72ft-high gateway with fluted columns supporting a simply massive pediment into which the word 'Euston' was emphatically lettered. This loud trumpeting welcome to the somewhat less classical train shed behind was itself heralded by two pavilions on the Euston Road, replaced in 1869 by pedimented lodges by James Stansby. These neglected little buildings in Portland stone, with their relaxing Greeks sculpted by Joseph Pitts, are now the only survivors here from a more gracious age of railway travel.

On the concourse of the present terminus we can stare at the continually changing names on a huge digital destination board. But in 1869 the London & North Western Railway was sufficiently confident of where it was going that it cut far-flung destinations into the quoins of the lodges. (The railway was equally confident that its name wouldn't change every year to something like BrumRail, so a sculptured monogram of its initial letters was included.) The incised lists optimistically included stations not actually on the railway's lines such as Cambridge and Cork, and out of 72 names only 37 were on anything like a direct route.

THE RESTORATION
OF THIS SHELTER
IN 1989 FOR THE
**CABMEN'S SHELTER FUND**
WAS PROMOTED BY THE
**HERITAGE OF LONDON TRUST**
WITH GENEROUS ASSISTANCE FROM
THE CITY OF WESTMINSTER,
ENGLISH HERITAGE,
BARCLAYS HOTELS GROUP,
THE HEDLEY FOUNDATION,
RTZ,
THE SWAN TRUST
AND
THE SEVEN PILLARS OF
WISDOM TRUST

## CAB SHELTER, TEMPLE PLACE   ⊖ Temple, Warwick Avenue

We so very nearly lost these curious structures from the London streetscape. They were the result of a rare philan-thropic gesture by a newpaper editor in 1875, when Sir George Armstrong of *The Globe* founded The Cabmen's Shelter Fund with the Earl of Shaftesbury as its president. The initials 'CSF' can clearly be seen amongst the fretwork decorations under the eaves. The idea was to provide cabmen with a refuge where they could 'obtain good and wholesome refreshment at very moderate prices'. Alcohol wasn't served so there was the added benefit that your cabbie might be sober. Of course, when they appeared this was the horse-drawn age and the Metropolitan Police agreed to their erection on the streets provided they took up no more space than a horse and cab.

Sixty-one shelters were built, costing about £200 each. Thirteen still exist – including this example at the back of Temple Underground Station – all identical kit-form structures with timber-framed walls, tongue-and-groove panels, a felt-clad roof lined out with bright terracotta ridge tiles and a little lead-capped ventilation cupola. The CSF still exists and the shelters are now Grade II listed, with a number of bodies (including English Heritage) helping with their restoration and maintenance.

I was made very welcome inside one that sits next to Warwick Avenue tube station, where everything is designed to maximise on the limited interior. I particularly liked the range of sauces available and the microwave oven slung up out of harm's way like a hotel bedroom TV, for which at first glance I did in fact mistake it.

**BLACK ROD'S STEPS, HOUSES OF PARLIAMENT**  ⊖ Westminster

To avoid getting a severe crick in your neck, the best way to view this little pavilion is
with a pair of binoculars from the other side of the Thames, or better still from a boat.
The parliamentary official Black Rod has little to do with them; the steps are named after
Black Rod's Garden from which they lead, and are part of alterations made to the
embanking wall of the Houses of Parliament in 1860. The pavilion is only a porch, so I
imagine it acts as a glorified bus shelter for river passengers. Apparently a peer getting
married within the Palace of Westminster can use the steps to make good his escape
(presumably with his new wife) and pupils from Westminster School row up to them
once a year to partake of a cream tea on the House of Lord's terrace.

### GARDENER'S HUT, LINCOLN'S INN

⊖ Chancery Lane

Lincoln's Inn is where you come to have your pockets well and truly shaken out by lawyers. As they brush their wigs and adjust their club ties they can look out of their thinly-barred Georgian windows at the well-manicured lawns and gardens. Queen Victoria decided to visit Lincoln's Inn in 1852; in the resulting panic money was found to build a hut for Mr Temple, the gardener. And what a hut. Mr Temple must have felt like keeping his hoes and rakes in velvet-lined cases in this magnificent red-bricked pavilion with its stone relief coats of arms and crow-stepped gables.

## REGENT'S PARK LODGES, MARYLEBONE ROAD ⊖ Regent's Park

Architect John Nash had a vision for London that in full flow would have connected the Regent's palace at Carlton House (pulled down in 1829, the site marked by the Duke of York's Column just off The Mall) with a park in Marylebone, now known as Regent's Park. Not much of his dream exists today. There are bits and pieces around Regent Street, of course, but after his plan failed to bear any really positive fruit he concentrated his efforts at the Regent's Park end.

At the top of Portland Place he planned a circus that would have had an inner as well as an outer ring of houses. The Napoleonic wars and his builder's financial difficulties resulted in only the southern half of the outer ring being completed, but the revised plans gave us these little Greek lodges. Built in 1823–5, two are at the northern corners of Park Crescent, with the two opposite them acting as full stops to the southern ends of Park Square. They are identical and each pair is joined along the roadside by equally identical railings and shrubberies. So like a mirror-image are they, I once came out of the adjacent Regent's Park tube station on a dark rainy night and ran all the way to Baker Street before I realised I should have gone in the other direction to Euston.

## QUEEN ANNE'S ALCOVE, KENSINGTON GARDENS ⊖ Lancaster Gate

This triumphal garden building by Wren is an architectural rarity. Like so many of London's curiosities, Queen Anne's Alcove has moved: from the opposite side of the park to a position where it turns its back on the Bayswater Road by the Marlborough Gate. It had become a haunt of 'undesirable personages' at its original site. Certainly there was enough room for them.

This oversize summer house was built in 1706–7 and, with its towering Corinthian columns and awe-inspiring curve of wood panelling as a back rest to the seat, it almost seems out of scale here in the park. Perhaps it would have been more at home at the end of a three-mile avenue on a Norfolk estate, flanked by dark Scots firs.

## CORAM'S FIELDS, GUILFORD STREET
⊖ Russell Square

Nobody cared much for illegitimate babies in the 18th century, particularly if they were poor, and their pale corpses would often end up discarded like so much unwanted refuse on rubbish tips or even more casually dumped at the side of the road. This appalling state of affairs did not go unnoticed, however, and a glimmer of hope for foundlings came with the red-coated Captain Thomas Coram, who was determined to build a foundling hospital.

George II was moved enough to sign a charter, George Frederick Handel gave his royalties from *Messiah* and William Hogarth designed a letterhead for Coram's fundraising. In 1740 the hospital's committee voted that 60 children be immediately offered places in the new building to be erected here in Holborn.

Coram's hospital was demolished in 1926, the empty space now appropriately a children's park. Almost all that survives, of the exterior at least, is the range of little buildings along what is now Guilford Street, including this stone niche where desperate mothers could leave their unwanted, or at least unsustainable, babies. On its opening day, 2 June 1756, 117 wriggling infants were left in this alcove. By the end of March 1760, no fewer than 14,934 babies had been abandoned here.

## TOOL SHED, SOHO SQUARE (left)
⊖ Tottenham Court Road

In the summer months the turf of Soho Square is difficult to see for backpackers and their backpacks. They lounge in various positions around this quaint pseudo-Tudor building that is about as incongruous here as a Canary Wharf tower would be in the centre of Stratford-upon-Avon. The centre of the square has been marked in the past by a statue, fountain and flower bed, until over 100 years ago architect S J Thacker brought this little piece of a Grimms' Fairy Tale to the heart of Soho. It is now a tool store and place of refuge for the park keeper.

big animals, small people

## THE LION BY WESTMINSTER BRIDGE, LAMBETH ⊖ Westminster

This white Coade stone lion stares imperiously out at Lambeth, an Aslan-like figure impervious to the tawdry plastic souvenirs being peddled around his plinth. Coade stone isn't really stone at all, but a ceramic substitute that is so realistic Robert Adam used it extensively for the exterior detail on his domestic façades. It was manufactured in Lambeth from 1769 until 1821, initially under the auspices of the firm's eponymous founder Eleanor Coade. Its unique selling point was that delicate decoration could look as if it had been individually carved when in fact it was mass produced, a great boon for the builders and architects of a rapidly-expanding London. So the lion is in fact an immense piece of pottery. We are often told that the 'recipe' for this magic substance was lost sometime after the manufacturing process was moved out of London to Stamford in Lincolnshire, but the British Museum has now apparently successfully cracked the Coade Code.

But this isn't the only deceptive thing about this magnificent beast. Far from being a gung-ho statement about Britain's burgeoning empire or a celebration of the arrival of a new queen, it is in fact a brewery trademark. Sculpted by W F Woodington in 1837, it is the largest of three red-painted lions that once padded around the skyline of the Lion Brewery that stood a little further downstream by the Charing Cross railway bridge. The brewery was blitzed in the war and after the area was cleared in 1950 for the Festival of Britain the site was occupied by the Royal Festival Hall. Mr Woodington – who was also responsible for the sinister leonine head of Joseph Paxton that glowers over the site of his most famous creation, the Crystal Palace – thoughtfully carved his initials and the exact date, 24 May 1837, on one of the lion's paws. Less than a month later, Victoria succeeded to the throne.

## THE CRYSTAL PALACE PREHISTORIC MENAGERIE, THICKET ROAD, SYDENHAM

≷ Crystal Palace

The original prehistoric animals that were placed on this Sydenham hillside when the Crystal Palace was re-erected here in 1852 (see p 95) have now been restored, painted and given fresh new ferns to tear away at. The mastodon was so big that the Victorians did what they always did when confronted by something big and exciting: 21 of them sat down inside it to have dinner.

Together with a few newer friends they line the bank of a small lake, edged with thoughtfully placed paths that facilitate good views of them munching and silently roaring up into the trees. I imagine that most people bringing their children here (and what a wonderful outing) don't realise that the original creatures are over 150 years old and not some *Jurassic Park* spin-off to feed the current dinosaur craze. These pale green creatures with their baleful lizard eyes are a small but memorable remembrance of what once stood here on one of London's highest points, a site that still mourns the extinction of another dinosaur, the Crystal Palace.

## ALBERT'S ELEPHANT, KENSINGTON GARDENS

⊖ South Kensington (Science Museum exit)

The Albert Memorial deserves a very large book all to itself, preferably one bound in red Moroccan leather with gold clasps engraved with acanthus leaves. We will all be familiar with this paean to Queen Victoria's consort, architect George Gilbert Scott's soaring, Gothic celebration of just about everything in Albert's life. Although larger-than-life, the sculptural groups on each of the extreme corners can often be overlooked as the eye is continually drawn in under the vast canopy to where Albert sits in gilded splendour.

Each of them deserves attention, symbolising as they do the four continents that contributed so much to the Great Exhibition of 1851, each group surrounding a representative animal. So the Americas have their bison, Europe a bull. Africa nearly got a lion but, in case there was confusion with the British lion, it was changed to a camel. But best of all, and the one most admired by Victorian critics, is John Foley's *Asia* on the south-east corner with its depiction of the Indian elephant. The kneeling position was intended to suggest 'the subjection of brute force by human intelligence', so no pussyfooting around there then.

The white campanella marble gives the elephant an almost eerie, other-worldly look. I don't know how many people had seen an elephant by this time, but they certainly hadn't seen a white one unless it was in a mission hall jumble sale. This pale pachyderm must have set a few fans fluttering nervously, particularly by the light of a full moon, with the thought that the subdued animal may slowly get up, scattering the rest of the Asia group down on to the steps in order to harrumph off into Knightsbridge.

## HOLBORN VIADUCT  ⊖ Farringdon

Wander up the middle of Farringdon Street from Ludgate Circus and you are walking above the gloomy subterranean reaches of the Fleet River. High up in front you will see William Heywood's ebullient cast-iron bridge, built in 1863–9 to provide much-needed relief to the highway that had to dip steeply down and up again across the valley between Holborn and the City. From the road below the decorations appear as standard Victorian embellishments, much gilded ironwork building up to the City's heraldic badge. Along the parapet are four bronze statues of an 'improving' nature: Commerce, Agriculture, Science and Fine Art.

At each corner of the bridge four Italianate 'step' buildings housed stone staircases that allowed access to the roadway above. Two of them survive on the south side, ghostly forgotten places that reek of the past (and much else). On the road above, the perspective changes completely and it's like going behind the scenes at a particularly colourful play. On each corner are fearsome winged lions that wouldn't be out of place as gargoyles on a Gotham City skyscraper, but if you come onto the bridge from Holborn, as I did, the real oddities appear to be just below the parapets. Angry silver griffins flick their fiery tongues at a black-winged helmet that stares out sightlessly over Smithfield on one side and down to Ludgate Circus on the other. Utterly surreal until you realise that you're looking at the backs of the coats of arms.

**ST ANDREW HOLBORN, HOLBORN VIADUCT**

⊖ Farringdon

In the late 17th century there appears to have been a fashion for brightly-painted figures to promote charity schools. There are a couple in Rotherhithe on the Peter Hills School and these two that originally started out on the wall of the Parochial School in Hatton Garden. Now they stand either side of the west door of St Andrew Holborn – rebuilt by Wren in 1685 – which now advertises itself as 'probably one of London's best kept secrets'.

### THE GEORGE, STRAND ⊖ Temple

This lugubrious monk with his barrel of Bass – a colourful variant on
the medieval gargoyle – earns his drink for doing service as a corbel
on the fascia of The George pub opposite St Clement Dane's church.

### TWININGS, STRAND ⊖ Temple

This is the original Twinings shop, where you can still buy fine teas
(including the evocatively named 'English Breakfast', so redolent of a
crisply folded newspaper and the aroma of pipe tobacco) and fruit
and herb infusions. The two Chinamen and the lion are made from
the ubiquitous Coade stone and have lounged about here above the
shop door since 1787. The lion is a reminder that the original shop
was at the Sign of the Golden Lion. Richard Twining had persuaded
William Pitt to reduce the Surrender Tax on tea, which at this time
was exclusively imported from China, hence the presence of the
beautifully painted Chinamen.

after life

## MERCANTILE MARINE MEMORIAL, TRINITY SQUARE ⊖ Tower Hill

Opposite the Tower of London is a classical temple by Edwin Lutyens in honour of the 'twelve thousand of the Merchant Navy and Fishing Fleets (1914–19) who have no grave but the sea'. Their names and vessels are recorded on bronze plaques covering the walls.

In the memorial gardens more names can be found, encircling a sunken garden and commemorating those lost in World War II. This monument was designed in 1955 by Sir Edward Maufe, the architect of Guildford Cathedral. Separating the columns of names are bas-relief panels of nauticalia, including this voluptuous mermaid combing her hair in true storybook fashion. I find her particularly extraordinary, not so much for her wanton pose but more for the mermaid details. Instead of the usual one-piece fishtail extending from the waist she has a pair of tails attached to each leg like piscatorial swimming flippers.

## THE SULLIVAN MEMORIAL, VICTORIA EMBANKMENT GARDENS ⊖ Embankment

Arthur Sullivan's head looks out over the gardens as if utterly unaware of the girl leaning against his plinth. She is so distraught she appears to have lost most of her clothes. The memorial was designed by Sir William Goscombe John in 1903 and celebrates one half of the prodigiously popular comic opera duo Gilbert and Sullivan. I think it's one of the most erotic figures to be seen in memorial sculpture and it inspired the contemporary rhyme:

> Why, O nymph, O why display
> Your beauty in such disarray?
> Is it decent, is it just,
> To so conventional a bust?

I quite fancy something like it for my memorial, should people feel so inclined.

## THE NECROPOLIS RAILWAY, WESTMINSTER BRIDGE ROAD ⊖ Lambeth North, ⇌ Brookwood

Even on the sunniest day, this building still manages to give me a slight chill. The imposing edifice of red brick and terracotta is all that remains in London of a railway that once ran funeral trains out to a simply prodigious cemetery amongst the pines of west Surrey.

In the mid-19th century the London Necropolis & National Mausoleum Company provided an answer to the very pressing problem of a fast-growing population and the resulting lack of burial space for the dead. Two thousand acres of land were purchased from Lord Onslow next to Brookwood Station to the west of Woking and a branch line was brought off the main London & South Western Railway (LSWR) to run through sombre Wellingtonias to two cemetery stations.

On the one hand it was an eminently practical solution of great appeal to the shareholders, but on the other it was also the ultimate realisation of the Victorian idea of the Railway of Life, where the progress of an individual could be marked out on routes that ended in the termini of either Heaven or Hell, with only Calvary Junction offering a safe ticket to the former. I think this is the reason why so many vicars double-up as train buffs.

In 1902 this new building was opened at 121 Westminster Bridge Road. The horse-drawn funeral corteges would clatter in from the road to check in at the cream- and dark orange-tiled office, which can still be seen through the steel railings that now close off the entrance. They would then turn sharply to the left where lifts and stairs carried the parties up to the simmering trains that waited on each side of a glass screen separating the first- and third-class platforms. There were waiting rooms and a chapel, but inevitably the coffins, each with an LSWR (and later a Southern Railway) ticket, were slid onto partitioned racks in the specially constructed hearse vans and the mourners silently settled themselves down into the comfort of the buttoned carriage cloth of their compartments. Then the trains would chuff out on a short length of track that joined the main lines just as they emerged from the Waterloo train shed, gathering respectable speed for the sorrowful miles out to Brookwood.

Leaving the main line, the funeral train ran through the laurels and conifers to the North Station for 'Roman Catholics, Jews, Parsees and other Dissenters' and thence by a level crossing over the Pirbright Road to the Anglican South Station. This is the only place to see any appreciable remains of the Necropolis Railway. The station buildings have disappeared, but the platform is still there. If you look very carefully you can see amongst the ferns an appreciable dip in the platform edge that facilitated the removal of coffins from the lower racks. The mortuary chapel is now the home of Russian Orthodox monks, whose privacy should be respected but who are very kind and helpful. This thought-provoking railway carried its last coffins and passengers in April 1941, when, after a few near misses, the station was bombed by the Luftwaffe, never to reopen.

S GRIFFIN
· LABOURER
2 · 1899 | IN A
XPLOSION AT A
SUGAR REFINERY
LLY SCALDED IN
NG TO SEARCH
HIS MATE

WALTER · PEART DRIVER
AND HARRY · DEAN FIREMAN
OF THE WINDSOR · EXPRESS
ON JULY · 18 · 1898
WHILST BEING SCALDED & BURNT
SACRIFICED THEIR LIVES IN
SAVING THE TRAIN

NDREW FORD
ETROPOLITAN FIRE
AVED SIX PERSONS

AMELIA KENNED
AGED 19 ·
DIED IN TRYING TO

## POSTMAN'S PARK, KING EDWARD STREET &#x2296; St Paul's

This little oasis of green is located opposite the old General Post Office in King Edward Street. Once the churchyard of St Botolph's, Aldersgate, it became a quiet lunchtime place for postmen to open up their greaseproof paper packages of fishpaste sandwiches. It is still the location of a totally unexpected and melancholic set of memorials.

All along an eastward-facing wall are beautifully lettered ceramic plaques, protected from inclement weather by a lean-to loggia. Each plaque commemorates an act of bravery: not heroic deeds in battle, but simple acts of extreme heroism and self-sacrifice involving catastrophes like runaway trains and sinking ships. These commendations of ordinary people in extraordinary circumstances celebrate individuals like William Drake, who in 1869 averted serious injury to a lady whose horses became 'unmanageable through the breaking of the carriage pole'. The lady is anonymous; it's William's name that has survived. As has that of David Selves, who 'supported his drowning playfellow and sank with him clasped in his arms', and Amelia Kennedy, who died in a burning house in Stoke Newington trying to save her sister. Thomas Griffin died searching for his mate after an explosion in a Battersea sugar refinery.

The plaques were the inspiration of the Victorian artist G F Watts (the sculptor of *Physical Energy* for Kensington Gardens), who was particularly moved by the story of Alice Ayres, a live-in maid who successfully rescued her employer's children from a burning house and then died when she attempted to save herself by jumping from a window. He quite rightly thought that these acts of selfless bravery should be commemorated, but the idea didn't continue much after Watts' death in 1904. He designed the simple but beautifully effective lettering and decorations on the plaques, which were produced by Doulton in their Lambeth factory.

MARY ROGERS
TEWARDESS OF THE STELLA
MAR · 30 · 1899
ELF SACRIFICED BY GIVING UP
HER LIFE BELT AND VOLUNTARILY
GOING DOWN IN THE
SINKING SHIP

GEORGE STE
POLICE
DEC · 22 · 1899
THE ELEPHANT
HACKNEY WICK
TWO LIVES. W
FLAMES, SA
AT THE RISK

EDMUND EMERY OF
272 KING'S ROAD CHELSEA
PASSENGER ·

WILLIAM
BAYSWATER
RAILWAY C

ALICE AY
DAUGHTER OF A BRICKLAYER
WHO BY INTREPID
SAVED 3 CHIL
FROM A BURNING
IN URSULA STREET, B
AT THE COST OF HER O
APRIL 2

G GARNISH
A YOUNG CLERGYMAN
WHO LOST HIS LIFE
IN ENDEAVOURING TO
RESCUE A STRANGER
FROM DROWNING AT PUTNEY
JANUARY 7 1885

JAMES BANNISTER

### HIGHGATE CEMETERY, SWAINS LANE  ⊖ Archway

This is secret London, but a secret recognised by aficionados as one of the most beguiling cemeteries in the world. Many will know of its curious and sombre delights – particularly on the western side – from the late John Gay's stunning black-and-white photographs in his aptly named book *Highgate Cemetery: Victorian Valhalla*. This wilderness of graves, vaults and monuments is slowly emerging from the stranglehold of plants and undergrowth: angels peering down in benefaction through the leaves, faithful dogs sleeping and crying children clutching rustic crosses.

From Bayswater and Maida Vale, the funerals came: from Kentish Town, Camden, Belsize Park, St John's Wood. Bankers and their clerks, doctors, poets, grocers, grocers' boys: all were equal now as they made their final journeys up from the pigeon-haunted towers and steeples of the metropolis, the engraved glass hearses pulled by black-plumed horses nodding and snorting up through the dark shades of Swains Lane to this steep hillside to join Faraday, Galsworthy, Landseer, the Rossettis. And, in 1853, John Atcheler, horse slaughterer to Queen Victoria.

The paths twist and turn upwards from the buttressed turrets of the cemetery chapels, past countless leaning crosses and draped urns until an extraordinary sight starts to appear through the ivy. A tunnel entrance cut into the hillside is flanked by pairs of bulbous Egyptian columns; once inside, the gloom slowly dissipates to reveal rows of vault doorways on each side. The ground rises up to the light where a ring of sunken tombs – each with a classical or Pharaonic entrance doorway – is guarded over by the black silhouetted branches of a spreading cedar.

The Egyptian Avenue and Circle of Lebanon are the eerie showpieces on these 37 acres of Highgate Hill, established by the London Cemetery Company in 1836, but equal pleasures are to be found down amongst the trees and shrubs. The Friends of Highgate Cemetery have worked miracles in restoring so much for us to see, but jealously guard their demesne. The guided tour is the only way we can enjoy these things; I long for a time when we can sit here alone in quiet contemplation, as so many others were able to do in the past.

## GATE PILLARS, ST NICHOLAS'S CHURCH, DEPTFORD GREEN ⮀ Deptford

The original church was demolished and rebuilt in 1697, but it still retains the medieval tower. In the churchyard is a rare 18th-century example of a charnel house, a repository for old bones disturbed during interments, and inside the church are carvings attributed to Grinling Gibbons of *Ezekiel's Vision of the Valley of Bones*. He is also thought to have been responsible for the pair of gruesome death's heads on the churchyard entrance pillars.

And that was going to be all I could say about these particularly startling sculptures, until one day I was looking at William Hogarth's painting *Chairing the Members*. There in the background of a riotous mid-18th-century election scene is one of these pillars, or at least one very much like it, with a chimney sweep cheekily placing a pair of spectacles on the nose of the skull.

## WOMBWELL'S LION, HIGHGATE CEMETERY, SWAINS LANE ⊖ Archway

This benign lion sleeps amongst the dense undergrowth of the Highgate West Cemetery. The inscription tells us that George Wombwell was a menagerist, which perhaps sanitises his occupation as a ruthless and avaricious showman who toured the country with an exhibition of 'wild beasts'. It is indeed ironic that a lion was chosen to mark his tomb, since Wombwell was not averse to setting up gladiatorial combat between his two lions, Nero and Wallace, and slavering dogs. The general public had little opportunity to see exotic beasts and Wombwell was amongst the first to exhibit elephants, creatures that rapidly became the stars of his travelling show.

Twelve years after his entombment here in 1850, the Wombwell menagerie, now run by his widow, arrived in Leicester where a crippled and pregnant girl narrowly avoided being trampled to death by a parading elephant. Three months later she gave birth to a son, John Merrick, better known to us as The Elephant Man.

**SIR RICHARD BURTON'S TOMB, NORTH WORPLE WAY, MORTLAKE** ⇌ Mortlake

Portraits of Richard Francis Burton tend to show a rather cross-looking man with a big black crescent of a moustache. His achievements were legion; apart from learning 25 languages and 40 dialects he was one of the foremost Victorian explorers, travelling around and writing about Asia, Africa and South America. He also used his skills as a translator to give us what is still recognised as the definitive text of the *Arabian Nights*, the publication of the first unexpurgated edition causing the usual fainting fit Victorian scandal. His widow, Isabel Arundel Gordon, burned his translation of *The Perfumed Garden*, but redeemed herself by producing this startling and utterly original mausoleum for her husband on his death in 1890.

I found it on a dry, dusty summer day, the graveyard of St Mary Magdalene in Mortlake having more of the atmosphere of an Italian *cimitero* than a South London burial ground. Surely a more appropriate monument to an explorer couldn't be made: a life-size stone tent complete with

decorative fringing, moulded ropes and creases in the pretend canvas fabric. A crucifix is attached above where one assumes the entrance was and on my visit the cross was accompanied by a stuffed toy camel.

But the biggest surprise is round at the back, so incongruously near the back gardens of a terrace of houses. An iron ladder can be climbed up to a window let into the tent roof. When I got to the top all I could see was my reflection and that of the still trees above until I cupped my eyes to peer in through the glass. Immediately below I could see a small altar and the remains of votive lights. And then, there they were, Richard and Isabel on each side of the tent, resting as if they were on some bizarre camping expedition with their coffins resting on foldaway beds. Disturbingly, Isabel's coffin lid was very slightly ajar. Everything was dusted in an aching patina of great age and I left for a slow thoughtful walk back through the heat to Mortlake station.

# smithfield market

## SMITHFIELD MARKET, CHARTERHOUSE STREET ⊖ Farringdon

Smithfield is London's wholesale meat market, a nocturnal city of carcasses where one can eat steak in a pub at six in the morning. By midday most of the serious business of humping meat about is over, the loud hums of refrigerated vehicles and shouts from white-hatted butchers subdued until the next day, but at any time there is always the echo of William Hogarth and Charles Dickens. In greasy alleyways butchers still carry pink carcasses over their shoulders and wet pavements look as if offal has only just been swept out of sight.

It's not difficult to imagine the distant past here: tightly packed cattle being driven into pens made from wooden hurdles, the flies, the heat, the guttural shouts and red kites wheeling above it all. And from time to time, it would all be cleared away so that they could burn somebody at the stake. Stakes and Steaks: A History of Smithfield Market.

Of course, now there are those who think that this land is too valuable to be left alone and the snouts of property developers can be heard snuffling around amongst the pork chops and tripe dressers. Smithfield is the great survivor, a wholesale market still at the heart of the City, while other markets – for fish, fruit and vegetables – have now been banished to the fringes. If Smithfield goes, then nothing is safe. Do we really need yet another ghastly mix of moribund office accommodation, wretched 'retail opportunities' and greedily-priced flats with security gates?

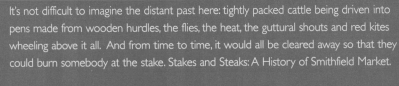

moving stories

## TEMPLE BAR, PATERNOSTER SQUARE

⊖ St Paul's

An extraordinary piece of the capital's architectural history sits lost in the Hertfordshire countryside. The Temple Bar marked the boundary between the cities of London and Westminster and was once as familiar and recognisable to Londoners as St Paul's Cathedral. This Portland stone gateway straddled the point where Fleet Street becomes the Strand, at the spot marked today by a fearsome dragon rearing up ready to blast his fiery breath at Westminster.

Christopher Wren is most likely the designer of this dramatic piece of Baroque, with its niches, statues and overflowing cornucopiae surrounding the central arch and the two dark and narrow pedestrian tunnels. Completed in 1672 it quickly became a focal point for ceremonies and processions and, this being the 17th century, was often embellished with the severed heads of traitors. As London's vehicular traffic increased, the Temple Bar became a noisy bottleneck and once the north side of the street was demolished to make way for the new Royal Courts of Justice its future was in jeopardy. It survived *in situ* until 1878, when the component parts were removed and stored in a yard off Farringdon Street. Ten years later brewer Sir Henry Meux purchased it wholesale and re-erected it as an eye-catcher at Theobalds, his estate near Cheshunt. His wife hid a time capsule amongst the stones.

That would have been the end of the story, except that now it is being dismantled again and moved back to London, where it will be on show again for the first time in over 125 years, reassembled in the new Paternoster Square next to St Paul's. Almost back home. And yes, they found the time capsule. Most of it was a fine mulch of 19th-century paper, but there were some coins and a piece of the *Sporting Times* for 7 January 1888 with the clearly discernible word 'Wizard'. Exactly the right word for a building that has magically appeared in three different locations in its lifetime.

**CRYSTAL PALACE, HYDE PARK**

⊖ South Kensington (Science Museum exit), Holme Fen Post: ⊋ Peterborough

To a Londoner walking through Hyde Park in the summer of 1851, the vast glass walls and curving roofs shimmering through the trees must have seemed like a building dropped, if not from heaven, then at least from another planet. Joseph Paxton's phenomenal Crystal Palace was home to the Great Exhibition, an extraordinary showcase for the burgeoning machine age that turned London – for that year – into the only place to be in the world. The glittering pavilions showed off everything from Bellhouse's Fireproof Doors for Warehouse Hoists to a stuffed cat playing a piano. *The Times* worked out that if you wanted to look at everything properly you'd have to come every day for an entire month.

As the echoes of the final visitors receded, plans were quickly implemented to move the Crystal Palace to a new home up on the crown of Sydenham Hill. However, there are at least two reminders of the exhibition that never made the journey into south London and therefore, by accident or design, missed being destroyed by the apocalyptic fire that engulfed the enlarged Crystal Palace on a November evening in 1936.

The original Coalbrookdale cast-iron entrance gates from inside the exhibition are now at the west end of the South Carriage Drive in Hyde Park. They once featured prominently in many engravings of the grand entrance, which was swung open by a Beefeater on 1 May 1851 for Queen Victoria, who was decked out in a pink silk dress embroidered with silver and studded with diamonds.

And out on a Cambridgeshire fen is probably the most curious reminder of this extraordinary glass palace. The Great Exhibition coincided with the draining of one of the last great tracts of original fenland, Whittlesey Mere, by John Lawrence. He picked up a cast-iron column from Hyde Park during the great dismantling and drove it through 22 feet of undrained peat to the underlying clay. The idea was to measure how much peat shrinkage would occur and by 1955 the column was 12 feet above ground. Today so much of the column – now called the Holme Fen Post – has been revealed that it needs a set of iron supports to stop it toppling over.

## MODEL DWELLING HOUSE, KENNINGTON PARK ⊖ Oval

Queen Victoria's consort, Prince Albert, was a prime mover in the whole staggering enterprise that was the Great Exhibition of 1851. It was a role he had always wanted, to be at the centre of things instead of hanging about on the fringes of his wife's responsibilities, and his input is still manifest in the buildings and ideas that grew up in the aftermath of the exhibition. We owe the Royal Albert Hall and the museums of South Kensington in part to his vision, but there is a much humbler building that he initiated, now forgotten in a south London park.

His 'Model Dwelling House' was one of the 1851 exhibits that could stand inclement weather and so, along with traction engines and awe-inspiring lumps of Welsh coal, it was exhibited outside the glass arena. It was designed around the Prince's ideas for workers' housing by Henry Roberts, the architect for the very worthy-sounding 'Society for Improving the Condition of the Labouring Classes'. The premise was simple: a group of four flats sharing a communal open-well staircase that became a feature of thousands of mid-Victorian flats. However, it didn't really help the poor. Flats like these were only affordable by comparatively well-paid artisans. The Prince's model dwellings were later taken down and moved to Kennington where they are almost completely hidden by trees, very appropriate for the present occupiers, the Trees for London office. As a result it's very difficult to stand back and appreciate the two-toned brick dwelling, so one should visit it armed with a copy of a contemporary engraving in one's pocket.

## CRYSTAL PALACE PARK, SYDENHAM ⇌ Crystal Palace

Sometimes we lose buildings and, because their ground plan is quickly built on, the spirit of their presence is taken away. The ghosts of others hang around for much longer if their space is unfilled; having seen it all my life I thought I still saw the sinister Gormenghast tower of Leicester City's General Hospital for months after it had been taken down. And here, overlooking south London and much besides, one of the largest and most impressive structures ever built in Britain is only ever a tiny stone's throw of imagination away from being rebuilt in the mind, soaring up again into the Sydenham skies.

On its removal from Hyde Park the Crystal Palace, which housed the Great Exhibition of 1851, was brought here the next year and re-erected and enlarged by half again. Two tall Italianate water towers were built by Brunel at each end and a series of terraces and steps led down to a vast park where ornamental lakes and ferny undergrowth were inhabited by huge figures of prehistoric monsters.

Eighty-nine fire appliances from all over London failed to stop the Crystal Palace from transforming itself into a twisted glassless frame on 30 November 1936, the night of its destruction by an apocalyptic fire that could be seen as far away as Brighton. All that's left is an empty space that takes ten minutes to walk down, the area still marked by terraces and steps, some on the higher level guarded by crouching sphinxes. Go down these grand balustraded staircases and you come to the bust of Joseph Paxton, the creator of the Crystal Palace, who turns his leonine head away towards the mediocrity of some modern sports buildings. His plinth is now used as a support for an electricity cable.

It would have been truly appropriate and wonderful if we could have celebrated another 150 years of technological advancement with another crystal palace of our own age on this airy site above south London, or at the very least erected again just a corner of the original to show the world what literal heights Victorian engineering was capable of reaching. But, just as the loss of the *Titanic* in 1912 presaged a history-changing war, so the destruction of the Crystal Palace not only heralded the even greater conflagration of the Second World War but finally drew a full stop to that amazing Victorian era that had – to all intents and purposes – still soldiered on into a century not its own.

**ALL HALLOWS CHURCH TOWER, CHERTSEY ROAD,
TWICKENHAM** ⇌ Twickenham

A 17th-century City church tower by Christopher Wren. In the suburbs at
Twickenham. The church of All Hallows was originally in Lombard Street, but
it became unsafe and was pulled down in 1938. The white Portland stone
tower was moved out to the Chertsey Road, a landmark to look out for
while coursing the string of roundabouts on the A316.

## BATTISHILL GARDENS, NAPIER TERRACE, ISLINGTON

⊖ Highbury & Islington

Walk down into the little sunken garden in Napier Terrace and one is confronted by a relief sculpture of flouncing Mercurys and naked men astride horses, which runs around part of the garden. This is another piece of London far from its original site. It's as if buildings explode and send all their constituent parts into some crazy orbit until they're drawn like a magnet to alternative resting places.

The relief was chipped out in 1842 by Musgrave Watson for the House of Commerce in Threadneedle Street and removed to University College when the building was demolished in 1922. This piece of early Victorian art – designed to impress stove-pipe-hatted financiers – was later brought down to earth in an Islington park for everyone to enjoy. The new setting is perfect: a magical backdrop to well-tended plants and a tiny pond that reflects the detail darkly amongst floating leaves.

## WELLINGTON'S STATUE, ALDERSHOT
⊖ Hyde Park Corner, ⇌ Aldershot

The Constitution Arch sits marooned on a traffic island, and while not quite an Arc de Triomphe it is at least a hub of roads and traffic in the same whirling, noisy spirit. Once again this is a London building that has moved, but there's more to the story than just relocation.

The arch once stood behind Decimus Burton's Hyde Park Corner Screen, a trumpeting exit from the park towards Buckingham Palace. Burton also designed the arch, but couldn't believe his eyes when he saw the sheer scale of the equestrian statue of the Duke of Wellington that was placed on top. It must have been the reverse of Spinal Tap's tiny mismeasured Stonehenge descending at the climax to their rock gig. Burton objected to it in the strongest terms and he felt so badly about it he even left money in his will to have it taken away. Finally the arch was moved to its present site in 1883 and Wellington was taken off his plinth. In 1912 Adrian Jones's more appropriately-scaled Quadriga was lowered into position.

Matthew Cotes Wyatt's immense statue was taken out to the Hampshire woods and erected on a bluff of land above the Royal Garrison Church of All Saints in Aldershot. When I first saw it a few years ago its vast scale was emphasised by the surrounding trees which grew right up to the huge pink sandstone base, with Wellington and his fine horse rising up like some mythical warrior giant arriving at a critical moment of battle. But this is army land and eventually some work detail was sent out to cut down all the trees around it and ring it with bollards painted Parade Ground White, removing all sense of surprise and awe from the prospect.

The statue is signposted and has its own car park, so providing you don't look overtly suspicious or have a mortar over your shoulder you are welcome to visit it.

curiouser and curiouser

## ELECTRICITY SUB-STATION, DUKE STREET
⊖ Bond Street

The whole rectangle of Brown Hart Gardens, off
Duke Street, is a raised, balustraded terrace on
rows of arches. At each end is a neo-baroque
pavilion, each with four decorated pedimented
sides below a flattened dome. Facing Duke Street
and Balderton Street are studded doors like prison
entrances, all the more forbidding to guard the
flashing amps and ohms within, for this is electric
land, a sub-station to power the Kitchen Aids and
plasma TVs of Mayfair.

Tiny signs on the doors tell us that these are still
the property of whatever the electricity board is
now called in London, but the buildings themselves
are not of the telemetric microchip age. When
they were built in 1905 by C S Peach they must
have been like Frankenstein's laboratory: massive
switch gear and dangerous dials, levers being pulled
by nervous technicians guiding their invisible
energies out into the surrounding streets to the
accompaniment of deep humming and the
occasional pale blue flash lighting up everybody's
faces. Probably.

## THE DIORAMA, PETO PLACE ⊖ Regent's Park

Before the Lumière brothers set the first cinema audiences screaming at the sight of a steam train hurtling towards them, showmen had contrived to produce bigger and more spectacular optical thrills for their customers. One of the most popular was the panorama, where one could see, for example, a bird's eye view of a vast landscape from somewhere like the dome of St Paul's Cathedral. Part of the dome would be constructed inside an open space to give the illusion of great height and an amazed crowd would see a cleverly-painted city stretching away to far off hills, to the accompaniment of sound and lighting effects to show extremes of weather that obviously included a very loud thunderstorm. This being 19th-century England the changing programmes would naturally include Biblical themes like Belshazzar's Feast and military topics like the Battle of Trafalgar.

Louis Jacques Mandé Daguerre moved things on, literally, with the invention of the Diorama. Designed for an audience of 200 the Regent's Park Diorama opened at a cost of £9,000 on 29 September 1823. Here skylights and shutters illuminated the front of a screen and rows of windows on the exterior let in daylight to the back. The audience looked at scenes (in all moods: fog, snow and ice, summer) as if at the end of a tunnel and every quarter of an hour a bell would ring and the diorama would appear to move out of sight, to be replaced by another. In fact it was the whole auditorium that was revolving onto the next viewing tunnel.

The Regent's Park building can still to be seen in Peto Place. It closed as a Diorama in 1851 and was converted to a Baptist chapel. The ground glass windows used for the lighting effects were swopped for ones with a more ecclesiastical flavour. It has subsequently had many and varied lives, including use as a rheumatic clinic. I went to a wedding reception here once and told Kinks frontman Ray Davis all about it. Between slowly munching his piece of cake and looking very glum (as Ray can) he muttered, 'Monument to some Victorian megalomaniac I expect.'

**AUBREY WALK, KENSINGTON**  ⊖  Notting Hill Gate

Sometimes curiosities can be little architectural details that enhance the façades of buildings, not in an overtly decorative way, but in creating something utilitarian and then making a feature out of it. There are two entrances to these workmanlike-homes in a back street of Kensington, one at ground level and one on the first floor reached by steps that turn and ascend within the ground plan. Light falls on the stairwell from an upper storey opening, but here it is also recognised that with steps it's important to know where you're putting your feet. So the ends of the risers and treads on what would be the darkest section are open to the outside, picked-out in brilliant white paint to create an admirable abstract design with the deep red brickwork.

**SAVOY STREET, STRAND**  ⊖  Charing Cross

Savoy Street is the only street in London where you must drive on the right. This short lane is a cul-de-sac off the Strand, in effect the driveway for the Savoy Hotel. It affords chauffeurs and cabbies the convenience of being able to open limousine and cab doors without having to walk around their vehicles.

## FIRE STATION, OLD COURT PLACE, KENSINGTON

 High Street Kensington

You really do have to make a detour to see this building, which is located in a little winding cut through from Kensington Church Street to Kensington High Street. Designed by the Fire Brigade Branch of the London County Council Architect's Department in 1905, it is from an era when even something as prosaic as a fire station was well designed. Back then fire stations were given a presence – even in a small street like this – that exuded authority and confidence. There are many beautiful examples from this age; in particular I tend to stand and stare a lot at an Arts-and-Crafts fire station in Euston, but the Kensington building is recounted here because it's the very last fire station to have used horses to pull the appliances. At one time 300 horses were kept in the stables, but at the end there were just two bay mares in service, Lucy and Nora. Their last fire was at Christmas 1921 and on their return they were greeted by sugar and carrots served on a silver tray.

## MERIDIAN STUDS, PARK VISTA, GREENWICH

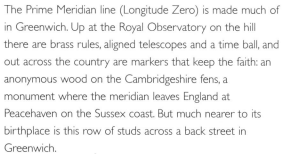 Maze Hill

The Prime Meridian line (Longitude Zero) is made much of in Greenwich. Up at the Royal Observatory on the hill there are brass rules, aligned telescopes and a time ball, and out across the country are markers that keep the faith: an anonymous wood on the Cambridgeshire fens, a monument where the meridian leaves England at Peacehaven on the Sussex coast. But much nearer to its birthplace is this row of studs across a back street in Greenwich.

In the late 1980s I walked down Feathers Place, the road you can see in the background, and saw a 'For Sale' notice outside a house that appeared to be bisected by the meridian, so I rang for details from the estate agent. Of course, they went on at great length about the fact that the front living room was in the west and the dining room and kitchen were in the east. I think this amazing fact resulted in a few bob being eased on to the sale price. Further on this invisible line crosses the Thames, where it is marked by a huge sign only visible to river traffic saying 'East/West'.

### THE MITRE TAVERN, ELY PLACE ⊖ Farringdon

Surely this is London's most hidden-away pub. Ely Place is slightly forbidding, a private road of terraced town houses jealously guarded by a porter in his little pedimented house at the entrance on Charterhouse Street. This is Crown property, but a curious anomaly means that Ely Place is technically in Cambridgeshire. For centuries the palace of the Bishop of Ely was here, until 1772 when the diocese found a more modish home in the West End and so flogged off the ground for new development.

In Elizabethan times some of the property was leased by the Bishop of Ely to Sir Christopher Hatton, who marked the boundary at one point with a cherry tree. This still forms part of the structure of The Mitre Tavern, as does a stone mitre from the original palace gatehouse. Sir Christopher, of course, gives his name to nearby Hatton Garden.

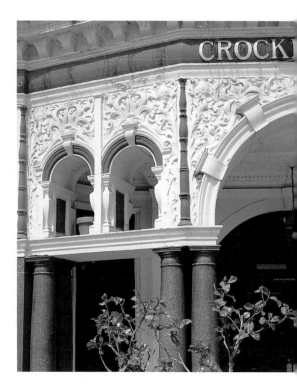

## CROCKER'S FOLLY, ABERDEEN PLACE

⊖ Warwick Avenue

In the late 1890s construction was underway on the last few miles of the Great Central Railway into London. Somebody told Frank Crocker that the new terminus would be somewhere near here, in quiet Aberdeen Place in Lisson Grove. So on the appropriate corner he built his railway hotel in 1898, a big airy hostelry that utilised everything out of the style catalogue: shaped brickwork, ashlared stone, white-plastered Moorish windows, marble bars, engraved glass and mahogany fixtures.

I have this heart-rending image of Mr Crocker going out to St John's Wood to watch the steam shovels digging out the embanking and navvies running about with barrow loads of ballast, his smile of satisfaction turning to an expression of horror as the railway failed to turn towards Aberdeen Place, but carried on for another three quarters of a mile into Marylebone. As the story goes he calmly went upstairs to his lincrusta-ceilinged bedroom and hung himself.

I'm sure the story has been embellished a bit over the last 100 years. Indeed Spike Milligan did a little film about it in which a steam train drew into Marylebone with Spike running behind it on the track, dressed as a waiter with a tray of drinks, shaking his fist and shouting veiled obscenities at the rear coach.

On my return visit I found to my dismay that it was closed and, after I'd convinced a passer-by that just because he saw me pummelling the brass hand plates on the door at eleven o'clock it didn't mean that I was desperate for a drink, he told me he thought there were plans afoot for a Lebanese restaurant. End of an era then, but something to talk about over the eggplant dip.

## ROYAL NAVAL COLLEGE GATES, KING WILLIAM WALK, GREENWICH ⇌ Greenwich

The gargantuan globes on the gate piers to the Royal Naval College are each six feet in diameter. Curling around their surfaces are iron bands that once represented celestial and terrestial movements. They were placed here in 1834 in commemoration of the world exploration undertaken in 1740–4 by Admiral George Anson, who while he was at it managed to lift half a million pounds off a Spanish galleon. There is something humbling in the sheer scale of the globes, as if at night they may slowly topple forward and rumble sonorously through the empty streets of Greenwich.

## ARCHWAY, HIGHGATE  ⊖ Archway

North London has many things that seem in our peripheral vision to cast metaphorical shadows, things that seem to whisper unspeakable truths. Passing through the area one is confronted with alarming corner turrets, which remain aloof and constant while parades of shops alter incessantly beneath them, forgotten tube stations hiding in tangled dells and the padlocked doors of soot-begrimed churches no longer mouthing the messages of misunderstood sects. And then there's Highgate, up on a hill, so like a London Transport poster, with its pubs on a tree-lined green, red telephone boxes and local shops. But with dark secrets on the edges – the clouds for its silver linings – found in the Hammer Horror Gothic cemetery halfway down Swains Lane and the stifling privacy of Holly Village behind its holly hedges at the bottom of the hill.

So if you're going to build a bridge in Highgate to fit in with all this, Archway does the job perfectly. By the early 19th century the dramatic increase in road traffic necessitated a route in and out of London that would bypass Highgate Hill, particularly in foul weather. Amazingly a tunnel was tried first, but this was quickly followed by the construction of Archway Road in 1812. The first bridge to carry the road over the ravine was an aqueduct-style affair by John Nash, later replaced in 1897 by this elaborate cast-iron arch designed by Alexander Binnie.

As I climb up from Upper Holloway, the bridge's sinister silhouette high above the carriageway never fails to darken my mood with unbidden thoughts of the once common suicides that fell like rag dolls from the parapet. One can only start to imagine the misery felt in those last footsteps tapping out along Hornsey Lane, followed by the screaming leap into oblivion high above the streets and smoking chimneys of the City.

## HOLLY VILLAGE, SWAINS LANE, HIGHGATE ⊖ Archway

This little piece of slightly disturbing Gothic is located at the bottom of Swains Lane. Probably it would be more at home forming part of a model village for a philanthropic country estate owner, but Holly Village still has all the right details: lattice fencing, elaborately rustic bargeboarding, diapered brickwork and statuary housed in pointed-arched niches on the gatehouse. And there is, of course, an inscription, which tells of the erection of Holly Village by A G B Coutts, the fabulously wealthy Baroness Burdett-Coutts who created this little enclave behind holly hedges in 1865. The 'village' is grouped around a little green and consists of only seven cottages and the gatehouse, which were built to house her elderly servants in a Picturesque ideal. It is intensely private, but enough can be seen from the road to get the general idea of what's going on.

## CROYDON ATMOSPHERIC RAILWAY, SURREY STREET ⇌ West Croydon

This set of brick buildings was once a waterworks. But big chunks of it didn't start out here and had a completely different function. The brown brick building with stone quoins has a date stamp of 1851 and was once the West Croydon engine house for an atmospheric railway.

The idea behind atmospheric railways was sound, but unfortunately the materials of the age didn't quite match the technology. The theory is that trains could be propelled by a piston slotted into a tube running between the tracks, from whence air had been extracted to create a vacuum. Air admitted back through a leather seal provided the power. Everyone would then fly along very fast holding on to their stove-pipe hats. Brunel had a go at Starcross on the Exe estuary and the only other English atmospheric railway ran from Croydon to Epsom; both were soon abandoned.

This peculiar railway connection would be enough to merit its inclusion in this book, but even as a waterworks it is not only a beautiful example of Victorian engineering with its polychromatic brickwork, oriel window and castellated tower, but equally remarkable is its survival in an area of London determined to recreate itself as downtown Houston.

**POLLOCK'S TOY MUSEUM, SCALA STREET**  ⊖ Goodge Street

Benjamin Pollock was a Hoxton shopkeeper who kept alive the
tradition of the toy theatre, and his shop had many illustrious
customers including Robert Louis Stevenson and Serge Diaghilev.
After his death in 1937, aged 80, his printing plates and printed
sheets were preserved until the 1950s when they were added to a
museum of Victorian playthings, and Pollock's Toy Museum was born.

Walking down Scala Street the museum is unmissable, but one
imagines a few double takes are made at this fabulous *trompe l'oeil*
shopfront, mixing as it does curiosities in a painted bow window
with real items peeping out from interior shelves. Particularly jolly,
and very apt, is the use of brightly coloured and tasselled theatre
curtains pulled back to reveal the show.

**PUNCH AND JUDY, CRYSTAL PALACE PARK, SYDENHAM**
⇌ Crystal Palace

These slightly sinister hand-painted wooden puppets have delighted
London's children – and adults – since the Restoration. They had
squabbled and beaten their way across Europe from Naples and,
although we perhaps associate these little candy-striped theatres
with seaside holidays, during the 19th century they had semi-
permanent pitches on London streets. They make numerous
appearances in the works of Charles Dickens, who vigorously
defended these fellow entertainers against those who thought all the
psychopathic behaviour morally reprehensible. This is David Wilde's
Punch and Judy Show under way in Crystal Palace Park, Sydenham.

390 Tufnell Park York Way King's Cross Euston Oxford Street

ARCHWAY STATION

ford Street
Aldwych **23**
Grove Sainsbury's

## THE ROUTEMASTER BUS ⊖ Oxford Circus, Bond Street

A bus? In a book about odd buildings and cast-iron street furniture? Well yes, because no book on London in the 21st century could possibly not mention it or, indeed, not make an impassioned plea for its survival. The Routemaster bus is as much a London fixture as St Paul's and Tower Bridge, and should be respected as such, not as a quaint museum piece but as a workhorse as vital as a black cab.

The Routemaster was born out of the need to replace London's trolleybuses, and the result, after two years of harsh testing, drove out onto the capital's streets in 1959, the same year as the Mini. And it's just as much of a design classic. The design brief was as it should be, to build a bus that was right from everybody's point of view: the operating managers', the drivers' and, of course, the passengers'. Weight reduction came with its aluminium body styled by Douglas Scott, retaining the isolated driving position that means better visibility and no distraction from passengers (thankfully Routemasters still need conductors). Comfort came with independent front suspension, shock absorbers and warm air heating, features hitherto only found on cars.

It is a bus designed specifically for London, not like the off-the-shelf varieties we have today. By 1968, 2,760 had been made and passengers, drivers and conductors all loved it. And still do. Of course something so good has to be continually threatened with extinction, but the Routemaster still hangs on in there because it's quite simply the best bus London ever had.

EU regulations are continually thrown at it (how, they argue, in our wondrous health and safety culture, can you have an open rear deck from where all the passengers might fall off onto the road?) and committee after committee mistakes its superb design for sentimental nostalgia. Hasn't anyone looked at the London taxi lately? Here is the perfect example of how a piece of public transport can meet all the bureaucrats' dreams and yet still retain all the features we love about black cabs. The Routemaster can survive as well if we all put our hands up for the 'Push Once' stop button and put a brake on those who would consign it to the scrapyard.

# SELECT BIBLIOGRAPHY

Below is a selection of books that I have found very helpful in my research and deliberations. Many will unfortunately be out-of-print, but all are worth seeking out.

Barkshire, P 1987 *Paul Barkshire's Unexplored London*. Lennard Publishing

Barkshire, P 1989 *Paul Barkshire's Other London*. Lennard Publishing

Bushell, P 1983 *London's Secret History*. Constable

Clarke, J M 1988 *The Brookwood Necropolis Railway*. Oakwood Press

Collins 2003 *London Street Atlas*. Harper Collins

Davies, P 1989 *Troughs and Drinking Fountains*. Chatto & Windus

Duncan, A 1995 *Secret London*. New Holland

Fletcher, G 1962 *The London Nobody Knows*. Hutchinson

Hessenberg, I (ed) 1986 *London in Detail*. John Murray

Jackson, P 1951 *London is Stranger than Fiction*. Associated Newspapers

Jackson, P 1953 *London Explorer*. Associated Newspapers

Jones, E and Woodward, C 1983 *A Guide to the Architecture of London*. Weidenfeld & Nicolson

Leapman, M 2002 *The World for a Shilling*. Headline

*London Everyman Guides*. Everyman

Pearman, H 1951 *Curious London*. Farmer & Sons

Pevsner, N et al *Buildings of England series, London volumes*. Penguin

Rocque, J 1982 *The A to Z of Georgian London*. London Topographical Society

Sinclair, I 1997 *Lights Out for the Territory*. Granta

Sinclair, I 2003 *London Orbital*. Penguin

Snowdon and Headley, G 1999 *London Sight Unseen*. Weidenfeld & Nicolson

Stamp, G 1984 *The Changing Metropolis*. Viking

Trench, R and Hillman, E 1984 *London under London*. John Murray

# ACKNOWLEDGEMENTS

Many kind people have helped me with this book, with suggestions, information, help, editing, designing or by just being there. I am particularly grateful to Iain Sinclair for his opening words and understanding of these things.

Thanks to: René Rodgers, Val Horsler, Rob Richardson, Robin Taylor and Margaret Wood at English Heritage, Chuck Goodwin, Lucy Bland, Stephen Twining, Martin Coulthard, Bruce Harding, Biff Raven-Hill, Jennie Browning, Richard Gregory, Ana Williams, Philip Wilkinson, Mike Goldmark, David Ellis, Rupert Farnsworth, Carl Warner, David Stanhope, Margaret Shepherd, Leigh Hooper, Misha Anikst, Anne-Marie Kerrigan, John Richardson, Christine Beckwith, Friends of Highgate Cemetery, Keith Slater and Alan Cook at the City of Westminster, Tom Wareham at the Museum in Docklands, Hugh Jenkins at the Museum of Garden History, the good samaritans in Greenwich Park who shared their ice cold orange juice with me on a particularly hot day, armed policemen in Kensington and many unidentified cabbies, particularly those whose tea break I interrupted in Warwick Avenue.